OPENLY DIVINE

INSPIRATION
FOR
THE CONSCIOUS CREATOR
IN US ALL

By Jill Renee Feeler

©Jill Renee Feeler and Beacon for Lightworkers LLC
Publisher: Platinum Age Press
www.theplatinumage.com

ISBN-13: 978-0615921129
ISBN-10: 0615921124

Artwork: Diane Lynn Hix ©SeaAngel12
www.seaangel12.com

Book Cover & Inner Layout Design by Andrea L.
eBookSmithy@gmail.com

———⟨⟨⟩⟩———

What will the future hold? What will happen? What will we Be? Look with-In. The answers are personal, quantum and result in aligning ourselves with various timelines and possibilities for experiencing. Access Your Light of God at Your Core. Look not for predictions, but for encoded memories and stored light codes of what You Desire. What do You want The future/Your future to Be? What do you Want to happen? What do you Want to Be? And so it is.

———⟨⟨⟩⟩———

———⟨⟩———

Align with these vibrations and frequencies in this now moment and in all aspects of your Be-ing, nurture them, support them, amplify them, to set in motion Today the Reality of Joy, Love, Peace for Self and for all who choose the same. In this invaluable process, We are creating an energetic grid of expanded vibrational states of being. This process changes the Game on Earth, Shifting an Age for Self and for all.

———⟨⟩———

As an aspect of God, you, too are inherently Glorious. To own this eternal Glory need not lead one into feelings of superiority. A sense of inner glory is expansive in Light when it is sufficiently aligned with the inner gloriousness of all of humanity, and indeed all life, all that Is.

———◆———

There IS an overall Divine plan for Earth's and humanity's evolution and You are part of it. I know this... because You are here.

———◆———

This truth is inherently empowering, further tuning you into your Light to absolutely flood all your experiences, all your interactions, all your relationships. This Light is not from outside of you, but rather it is the Core essence of who and what you Are. Light flows from within the core of your being, rooted in your inherent, eternal Connection to your Expanded Self/Source Creator/God.

❦

Since you have chosen to experience this Shift from
the human form, it is very helpful to allow a truth
that fosters an authentic love for humanity. Without
that love for humanity you are limited in your ability
to truly feel the depth of love that Source Creator has
for you in your human form.

❦

⸻ ❧ ⸻

Can you feel the power of that energy? Imagine
what Creator ability you are tapping into from that
vibration. It is Grand and Limitless, aligning you
powerfully to your own God frequencies. From this
vibration of love, we are sufficiently empowered
to fulfill the dreams of humanity, by fulfilling our
dreams for ourselves, rooted in love, joy and honor
for self and others.

⸻ ❧ ⸻

I am open to assistance from my God essence in utilizing the gift of today's frequencies and energy patterns to further access and allow my personal and unique connection to Source/God Consciousness. This connection is truly to Me, the infinite Me in my pure, complete whole-ness.

Our true nature as a Sovereign Being is Light. All
can be used to further our human experiences as/
into the whole-ness of the eternal Self. This gateway
is within our spherical personal energy fields,
underneath all the veils of Separation we allowed
ourselves to experience.

Each being will personally know their own Divinity in their own Divine time. It is quite liberating to know that accessing your Divine Within is not contingent upon others doing the same.

As eternal Souls, we are each Masters of Light. Our responsibility is to be our Light by restoring it in all facets of our personal lives. "I Am eternally Light, and I Am restoring Light to this human experience". As Souls, we Chose this experience, based on our love for humanity and for Earth. The Light of God within allows us to recognize the Sovereignty in all humans, even when they are not seeing it themselves. We assist self and others by re-membering our Sovereignty and by seeing the Sovereignty in all, opening the doorway for the overall expansion of humanity into its original Divine state. And so it is.

———✦———

Unconditional love is the root of all upliftment
and ascension. Expanding the field of possibilities.
Creating outcomes which benefit all, for the sheer
glory of the experience. Love. Love. Love. Without
conditions nor constraints. This we know as our
eternal Selves and this is what we are re-storing in
these realities of Earth. Love.

———✦———

———❖———

We are in the process of Re-membering our Mastery,
as a Sovereign being, an infinite Soul. Incarnations
amidst Shifts, as members of the Ground Crew,
are about re-membering the Light that we Are, and
Be-ing our unique Light of God to the best of our
abilities.

———❖———

—⋯≫⋯—

This internal, endless Source of Light with-In is the root of well being, love and off the charts joy. It is always available and yet we choose. We make choices amidst the Separation game that still remains on Earth. The more we anchor Our Light into our energy fields, throughout the vast and growing array of choices, the more centered and stable we will be as the Shift becomes even more intense. Expanding beyond the many veils of Separation, into the Light that we Are. Darkness is an illusion, an illusion offered by the Separation Game of Earth in a Dark Age Cycle. All that IS is Light. And I celebrate LIGHT in all ways that I can in this amazing, unique reality we call Earth. That is my purpose, my mission, my Joy.

—⋯≫⋯—

Real change need not be hard, just meaningful.
Being in a routine of change and exploration leads to
further trust, based on growing evidence that we are
actually powerful enough to respond in Love to any
and all situations and experiences. As we embrace this
pattern of change and expansive, progressive growth,
we facilitate upward spiraling patterns, in all facets of
our life. Divine evolution, consciously created by and
for humanity.

———◈———

It is our thoughts, our truths, and our belief systems
that help determine our energetic frequency, our
vibrational status, and thus the reality that we're
creating.

———◈———

My humanity is not a condition, an illness. My human state is an opportunity to express my unique aspect of God from within physical form, affecting and creating matter, energy, life from these wondrous Earthly realms. Feel the alignment of this truth with your Divine self. Each thought, truth and belief can further align us with our God essence or they allow us to continue to experience Separation; we choose and we experience accordingly. Dynamic truths and beliefs give us more permission to explore our Divinity. Explore. Discern. Consciously choose.

Our Creator power includes the ability to Be love,
to Be joy, right now, with exactly as things are. We
are un-conditional love applied on a more macro
level, to the Earthly realms. Looking beyond the
unconsciousness to see and know the inherent light
of God in all things, in all experiences. Free to know
Love in what Is. And Creating from that framework,
we are aligned with the eternal Love of God.

Make time with your Self through meditation and a
quieted mind, accessing further layers of your unique
Divine Within.

———◆◆◆———

Like the ultraviolet color spectrum that lies beyond
the human eye's ability to see, the frequencies of
the highest dimensions are beyond the reach of our
limited 5 senses. A vast, interdimensional array of
Light-based realms and realities await us from within
accessible through our higher/inner sensory awareness
system. Meditation is one effective way of activating
this system. The broader energy frequencies now
available on Earth are sufficient for each human to
experience their Authentic Self very naturally. We re-
train our selves to allow these light-based frequencies
into all states of human consciousness. This is human
evolution.

———◆◆◆———

From this vibration of love without condition you start creating in a whole new way. You experience matter in a completely unique paradigm. You bring the limitlessness of God into the physical realities where the bending of timelines, where the upgrading of physical matter becomes everyday experience. And yet that is not the goal. That is the outcome. Because this is not about trickery and ceremonies and games. This is about mastery sharing its mastery of love and wisdom with self and with others, out of the sheer joy of the experience.

———✦◈✦———

We've done this before.... many of us... Shifted Ages.

———✦◈✦———

This is no longer an intellectual process; it is about trusting Who and What You Are... Carefully chosen and voluntary members of a Ground Crew who embody amidst critical changes in various realities to set in motion the updated Design Plans for the Dawning Age. We don't pick members that start at square one... We pick those that have the Soul-level experience, Unity consciousness instincts of Love and Light pre-wired and pre-coded in every facet of your energy field. Know You Are Light. We don't have to make you into anything. We simply Ask you to Remember Who and What You Are so that You can Be this instinctual, Sovereign Master of Light that you Are. You aren't in class, Dear Ones. You've taught these Classes.

—⦿—

We are experiencing this beautiful yet strange physical reality, with carefully selected body suits. We are often led to Act. To Create. To Discern and then Move into new spaces, to align with our desired experiences. And it can take leaps. Trust your Self. It feels so good to try new things, new approaches. To create New Endings to old dramas.

—⦿—

Unity consciousness and authentic unconditional
love are easily accessible from the 5th dimensional
energy structure now fully available on Earth. This
is authentic freedom and liberation for Humanity,
beyond the polarizing views of us and them and good
guys and bad guys.

———◆———

At the fifth dimensional operating frequencies, you open the heart-centered consciousness to extremely vast truths that are beyond right/wrong, good/bad. It takes some personal shifting and yet it is extremely powerful, allowing the miracles of love and light to unfold with grace and ease in our personal lives. Fifth dimensional consciousness and above is still a rarity on this planet and yet we are growing (and glowing).

———◆———

One of the most powerful changes we can make in
our life is deciding now is our time to experience
well-being and thriving. Our beliefs very much
determine our reality. Believe in you and your ability
to thrive. Believe in others and the thriving of all.

———✦———

A key opportunity amidst this Great Shift is when we re-member the deepest levels of bliss and joy don't happen in certain locations, with certain people or in certain experiences... They are no longer conditional, at the mercy of factors beyond our control and authority. True bliss, real joy, cosmic love we know from home are natural, self-created energy patterns available through our Authentic Self in all ways of experiencing our humanity. Bliss and joy are Created from within.

———✦———

As you get more accustomed to tuning into your own broader, love-based frequencies, you recognize that Faucet of Love is inside of you. You turn it on or off at will based on where your consciousness is tuned.

The more we take personal responsibility for our energetic frequencies we re-member to work with our energy in this dynamic, empowering manner. Faucet of Love, Faucet of Light for Self and spilling into all grid systems of the Earthly planes.

Words cannot express the significance of who and what we Are. We each play a role in Shifting an Age, by Consciously Choosing Light, Love and our desired frequencies as eternal beings . Bringing Home home. Making it available for the collective on Earth by our making it real and practical in all facets of our personal lives.

For Ascension and further expansion of consciousness, many humans are ready to step further into Unity or Source Consciousness. This is not a blend of Light and Dark; it is only Light. The identity of Source Creator, God, is 100% Light, of which you are a valuable and precious facet.

Dark is simply separation from the Light that we Are,
as offered in a unique and special reality like Earth in
a Separation Age cycle. Truths, beliefs and thoughts
and a specially tuned set of frequencies play key roles
in creating an Age. To experience/create the Platinum
Age we are shifting into, it is necessary to adjust
one's truths, beliefs and thoughts, aligning them to
the dawning age and the underlying frequencies,
when one is ready to make this huge shift... Ages are
created by the Ground Crew experiencing a particular
reality, by each of us, adjusting our personal realities
through our truths, thoughts, beliefs. Are yours
supporting the Age of your dreams, or something
else? Choose consciously, as the Master you Are.

We have allowed ourselves the opportunity in
this time phase to experience and access Divine
frequencies, re-membering Unity Consciousness
from within our human forms by expanding what it
means to Be physical and what it means to be human.
This opportunity is such a gift, and we gift this to
ourselves.

Just as the universe is expanding and further experiencing itself, as infinite beings, there is no end to expansion. We are never "done"... and yet we are/ were always Light, experiencing ourselves in various realities and dimensional states of being. Amidst a Shift, this experiencing is very dynamic; quantum.

Allow You to Be. The more you bring your inner
Light to the surface of your human consciousness,
the more readily we upgrade all facets of the Earthly
realms into its Divine state. Your dreams, passions,
natural gifts and abilities assist in aligning you to
the unique role you were intending to play. As these
continue to evolve and expand, we upgrade what
is possible, further exploring our own infiniteness.
Enjoying the ride as masterful Souls who consciously
choose, adjusting to the flow of energies and our
Divine inner guidance system.

———⟨⟩———

We did not come to Earth to fit in, anywhere. We know that there is another way to be, without war, without famine and without hate. Trust your Self. Look within to find the very unique vibrations of Love that you desire. Be this Love, this authentic unconditional love of God that you Are. From that level of experiencing yourself, there is no wrong way to be you. Trust You. Always.

———⟨⟩———

Beyond the fight. Beyond the need or even desire
to be "right". Beyond any hate. Beyond the fear.
There is Love. Discern, everything, from the eternal
rationality that is beyond the brain, which is Love.

Openly Divine

ABOUT THE AUTHOR

———◆———

JILL RENEE FEELER is a futurist, writer, alchemist and inspirational visionary for beings across the globe seek-ing personal re-union with their expanded vibrational access, their God Consciousness. Jill has unique access through her Expanded Self to eternal wisdom of this Ascension Cycle and the Divine blueprints in place for this dawning Age. This access forms the platform she utilizes to guide and model the developing Divine Human experience, filled with a sense of wholeness, thriving, joy and most importantly, love without condition. Jill's service is activating, revolutionary and life-changing.

This inspirational book offers Jill's messages combined with the images of SeaAngel12, created to inspire you and assisting you in experiencing authentic joy and sense of thriving in your life.

"We are in the midst of a Great Shift of Ages, evolving into a stage of humanity that is abundant in love, in joy, in peace. Restoring a sense of balance and Divine purpose in our lives. This shift starts within each one of us. Many are feeling nudged, prodded or even launched into a deeper, more personal relationship with the Love and Light of the Universe, of God.

This Cosmic Light of God/Source Creator is within You. It is who You Are. We simply forgot; a key component of any Dark Age.

It is Time to re-member the gloriousness of who and what we Are: Light and Love of Source Creator, experiencing ourselves with-in a divine human bodysuit."

- JRF

ABOUT THE ILLUSTRATOR

—◆—

DIANE'S images have been a beautiful partnership to Jill's work since Jill launched her global broadcasts in Jan. 2011.

Fate brought these two together again and they continue to collaborate. Diane's art is a unique expression of Divine frequencies we know from Home, made manifest on Earth.

The mandalas seem to pulse and move as you experience them, assisting in activating ourselves at a cellular level to our inherent Divinity. The mandala's center often appears to continue infinitely, deeper to the truth of infinite Love and Light that is the core essence of You.

Combined with Jill's messages, these materials are activated for your continued frequency expansion.

"My vision for my art is that it will awaken a resonance of LOVE within your SOUL so that you may see things through eyes that bless."

- Diane Lynn Hix
www.seaangel12.com

www.ingramcontent.com/pod-product-compliance
Lightning Source LLC
LaVergne TN
LVHW010036070426
835513LV00005B/119